Life Is Full Journal

Journaling To Renew Your Heart and Mind

Cassandra N. Vincent

Life is Full Journal by Cassandra N. Vincent, Vincent Media & Consulting, LLC, Baltimore, MD.

www.cassandranvincent.com

Disclaimer: The author of this book does not provide medical advice or prescribe the use of any technique as a form of medical treatment for physical, emotional, or medical problems without the advice of a physician, either directly or indirectly. The intent of the author is to only provide information of a general nature to help in your quest for emotional and spiritual development. In the event you use any of the information in this book for yourself, which is your constitutional right, the author assumes no liability for your actions.

Acknowledgements

Thank you God for giving your only begotten son, Jesus, for me to have abundant life. Lord you are The One, The Only True and Living God. I am forever grateful for the gift of love that you are to me and that I am now able to give to the world. To my parents, Wallace and Joyce Vincent thank you for your love, your guidance, and support. Dad and mom thank you for being fruitful and giving me the gift of a Christ-centered home growing up. To my grandma, Alva J. Vincent, thank you for standing tall, because of you I am here. To my grandma Lillian Ashby and grandma Melinda Goines, I am eternally grateful for the garden you planted and the love that grew beautifully from it and produced my mother, my aunts and uncles and cousins.

To all of my family and loved ones, my beloved brothers and sisters, my dear friends, and those who have added to my life may God continually bless you.

Table of Contents

Introduction: Life Is Full Journal

Welcome to the Life Is Full Journal experience. A space where you will be inspired to embrace spiritual and personal transformation in your life. The Life is Full Journal provides you with reflection questions, writing prompts, and affirmations. The purpose of this journal is to encourage growth and create intentional time of reflection.

This journal is designed to support you in a number of ways. Mostly, it will support you as you emerge into new seasons of growth and personal transformation. Life is like a garden. Cultivating a full and happy life is much like gardening. Gardening can be a beautiful process. A process that sometimes is tough, requires work but brings about beautiful outcomes. A diligent gardner proudly gazes at their flourishing garden knowing that special care and attention was given to the things growing in the garden. As you use this journal, you are encouraged to incorporate it as you desire into your schedule. Consider using this journal during times in your life when you need to pause, increase your gratitude, unplug and create intentional moments reflecting on the beauty of who you are, the purpose you possess, and as a space for renewing your mind. This journal will help you identify areas where you are looking to grow more deeply and expand your vision for your life.

My hope for you is that by using this journal you will discover that you have all that you need to move forward, flourish, and grow in abundance. I pray that in the midst of planning and "goal-getting" that the Life Is Full Journal will provide a retreat for your mind and your soul. My desire is that you will be refreshed during the time of journaling and through the life-giving words found throughout the book. I pray that every person using this journal is inspired to live bigger and purposefully as God intended. So, take time to release worries and allow this time of connecting to God and writing your honest desires to open new chapters of breakthrough and clarity.

Blessings,

Cassandra N. Vincent

The Life Is Full Journal is designed to support you:

→   *Create new personal narratives and mindsets*

→   *Renew your mind and gain clarity*

→   *Increase gratitude in your life*

→   *Eliminate limiting thoughts and beliefs*

How To Use the Life Is Full Journal

It is highly recommended that you use the Life Is Full Journal as a companion to the "Life Is Full: Musings on the Beauty of Life, Growth, and Love" book. However, it is not mandatory. This journal was designed as free flowing for use during time of reflection. That means you may decide to start at the beginning of the book and work your way to the end. Otherwise, you may decide to make entries based on the writing prompt you need most on a particular day. The writing prompts and affirmations are written in a way that encourages you to set aside time for in-depth reflection. Taking purposeful pauses (taking time for calmness and meditation) can lead to further powerful moments of productivity because of the mental refresh associated with the practice. It is said that a person thinks on average over 70,000 thoughts per day. Just think about your thoughts. There is a portion of good thoughts, curious thoughts, negative thoughts, learning thoughts, unsure thoughts and those thoughts are non-stop throughout your day. The Life Is Full Journal is a resource to support you in "taking the pause" and to refresh your mind.

Additional recommendations for using Life Is Full Journal:

- Disclaimer: This book is not to take the place of any medical care you are under or any future care you may receive.
- Consider using this journal for the purpose of renewing your thoughts and replacing old unproductive thoughts.
- Consider using this journal alongside Bible scriptures.
- Consider using this journal for personal growth and development purposes.

However you decide to use this journal, remember it is designed with your success and growth in mind.

LIFE IS LIKE A GARDEN

Life Is Like A Garden

What grows in a garden? What grows in a garden depends upon what has been planted there. Some gardens are bountiful and some are not. Some gardens are well cared for and others are not. The difference between these gardens are the time, attention, and care given to them. The garden cared for will yield many great things, many wonderful experiences for its owner, and will have the ability to provide in abundance. Flourishing gardens take patience, focus, care, gratitude, pruning and seasons of growth and times of harvesting. Sadly, the other type of garden is the one abandoned. These gardens become unused dirt lots that sit with unused potential.

If life is like a garden, what do you want to grow in yours? What gifts are you using to grow your garden? What are you pruning and removing? Is your garden flourishing and abundant?

A wise gardener discovers the value in her land. She consistently tends to her garden. Planting, pulling, watering, and harvesting her garden. Repeating and adjusting in each season. The wise gardener values the abundance that flows from her garden.

What type of garden are you cultivating?

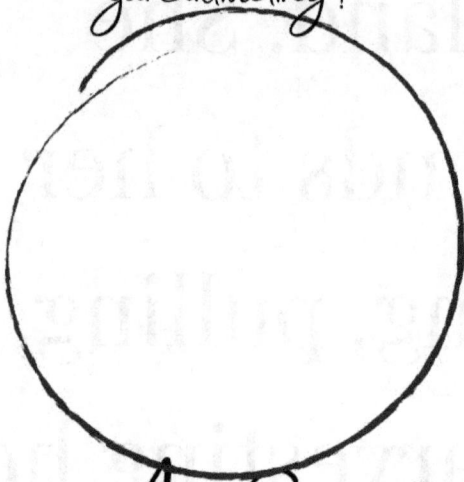

What things are you growing?

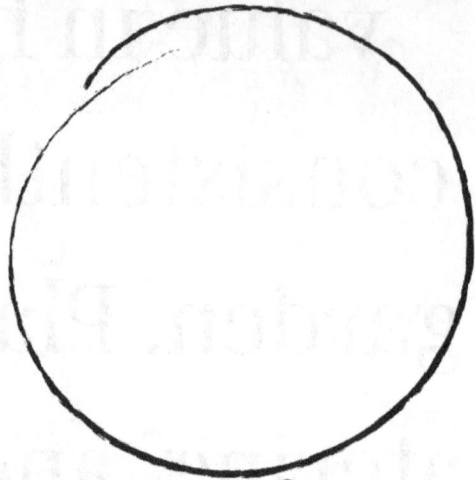

My Garden is filled with...

What are you watering your garden with? How often are you watering?

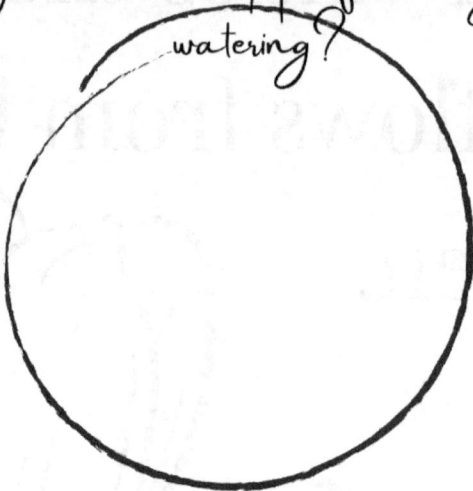

What needs to be pruned from your garden?

(Name your garden)

Life is Like A Garden: Cultivating A Beautiful Garden

Life is like a garden. There are many parallels to cultivating a beautiful life and gardening. Here are some below.

1. *Inspect your life. Inspect the land and soil where you are planting new seed.*

2. *Consider, prepare, and plan what you will grow.*

3. *Clear the area where you plan to grow your garden.*

4. *Work the soil. Cultivating the soil makes it ready for whatever seed you are sowing into the ground. Cultivating the soil provides for optimal growth.*

5. *Decide what you will sow and plant. Not every seed can be planted in the same soil.*

6. *Sow and plant in the right season.*

7. *Water your garden at the right times. Too little water or too much water can destroy what you planted.*

8. *Prune when needed. Prune routinely. Pruning is a tool it re-energizes and creates more growth.*

9. *Take care of your garden. Maintain and protect your garden. Keep your attention on it. A neglected garden cannot flourish.*

10. *Enjoy your garden. Whatever you have grown in your garden should be enjoyed and can be used to feed others. Harvest what you have grown. Give from the abundance of your garden. Then repeat.*

"Do life with joy."

Affirmations & Prayer for Growth

I am a success.

God created me for a great purpose.

The favor of God covers me like a shield.

God's blessings are all around me.

God is for me.

I choose joy.

My focus and motivation is love.

My heart is open to new beginnings.

Good things grow and multiply in my life.

I choose to seek out the best in situations.

I am purpose in living form.

I lack nothing.

I belong to God.

I am loved.

I agree with God.

I am flourishing.

Everything I touch prospers.

God desires for me to prosper.

Gratitude is my language.

I choose to see opportunities.

I am learning and growing beautifully.

My thoughts are lovely and good.

I am healthy, wealthy, wise, and my soul is prosperous.

I multiply. I leave spaces better than what they were.

My words create life and opportunities to experience greatness.

I give focus, love, and attention to the life God has given me.

Prayer

God here is my heart. I place my confidence in you. I agree with you, your thoughts, and what you say about me. Thank you for the opportunity to flourish in the purpose that you have created me for. Thank you for daily new beginnings. Thank you for liberating my mind, heart, and soul. I am open and ready to embrace all that you have planned for me. Amen.

What do you want your life to produce?

_____

_____

_____

_____

What legacy are you creating?

_____

_____

_____

What do you want your life to speak?

_____

_____

Life is like a garden, and I am filling my life, my heart, my mind with goodness. I am uprooting everything that does not support my growth.

- I am thankful for the love of God.

- I am thankful to be God's love on display in the world.

- I am grateful for peace, overwhelming, overflowing, peace.

- Goodness is abundant in my life.

- I am grateful for the opportunity to share the goodness that overflows from my life with others.

Today, in my garden I am planting and giving attention to:

_____

_____

_____

_____

Cultivate your life. Take note of what is growing there.

I am flourishing.

Below create and write your personal affirmation statements for various areas of your life. (health, finance, etc.) Write in the affirmative how areas of your life <u>are</u> flourishing. Although what you write may not yet be reality what you write will become your focus. What you focus on often becomes a goal.

_____

_____

_____

Below write your recent wins and things you wish to celebrate. (ie. lost weight, went to therapy, had hard conversations, etc.)

_____   _____

_____   _____

_____   _____

_____

_____

Affirmations are declarations and can be used to support an action toward a goal. An action first begins as a thought.

Life is like a garden. Many things can fill this space. As I reflect upon my life, I only want these things to grow in my garden...

_____

_____

_____

_____

- I am thankful for the right people and relationships growing in my life.
- I am thankful for productivity and making great use of time.
- I am thankful for love.
- I am grateful for the opportunity to grow and flourish in all areas of my life.

Today, I am taking time to see the opportunities to flourish in:

_____

I am creating a beautiful life.

Life is full of beauty.

- I am grateful for the opportunity to pause and reset my mind and heart.
- I am thankful for vision.
- My heart is open to see the blessings that surround me.
- I am taking note of the beauty that is in me and around me.

I am intentional and I take note of the many blessings surrounding me. I am blessed with:

_____

_____

_____

Today, I will care for myself by:

_____

_____

_____

Beauty is all around me and I choose to live a beautiful life.

Cultivating a life full of joy and happiness is a beautiful undertaking. Joy and happiness is designed for every soul.

- I am grateful for renewed hope.
- I am thankful for new thoughts.
- I am purpose, love, and joy in living form.

Life is like a garden. My life overflows with:

_____

_____

_____

I am thankful for:

I choose to live joyfully.

Life is about planting and cultivating goodness.

- I live in abundance and give from the overflow in my life.

- I am making powerful decisions today. I was created to dominate.

- I am building a legacy that will flourish for generations to come.

- I am cultivating great things in every area of my life.

Today, I will maximize the time I have been given by:

_____

_____

_____

I am thankful for:

_____   _____

_____   _____

_____   _____

Growth is beautiful and takes commitment.

- I embrace the beauty that comes with growth.

- I embrace the process of being and becoming who God says I am.

- I embrace the process of unlearning everything that does not align with who God says I am.

- I embrace the beauty of perpetual growth and development.

Today, I will look to grow in these areas of my life:

_____

_____

_____

_____

I am thankful for:

_____   _____

_____   _____

_____   _____

"The day you plant the seed is not the day you eat the fruit."

Today, [in my heart and mind] I am planting...

_____

_____

_____

_____

_____

My prayer today:

_____

_____

_____

Focus on your garden. Our gift back to God is what we do with what He has given to us.

Attention and care is given to what is valued.

My intention for today:

_____

I am grateful for:

_____

_____

_____

Today, I will grow in these areas of my life:

_____

_____

_____

My prayer today:

_____

_____

I value the time and gifts God has given me to use in this life.

Reside in the peace of God and nothing will overtake you.

My intention for today:

_____

I am grateful for:

_____   _____

_____   _____

I have great peace concerning this chapter and this season of my life. I celebrate my growth. I am cultivating my garden and giving it attention, not rushing, not pushing but making good use of the time that God has given me. I rid my heart of things that want to take the place of gratitude. Challenges may come, but they will not break me.

I have peace and trust that:

_____

_____

_____

_____

I choose peace over fear. I choose love. I choose joy.

I am growing wonderful things.

In my family & home I am growing and planting:

_____

_____

_____

_____

In my money and finance garden I am growing:

_____

_____

_____

In my health and wellness garden I am growing:

_____

_____

_____

In my relationships and life, I am growing:

_____

_____

I am thankful for:

_____

_____

I value time and the space God has given me.

Reflection

What am I feeling and thinking right now?

_____

_____

What lesson did I learn today?

_____

_____

How did I care for and/or invest in myself today?

_____

_____

What were my wins today?

_____

_____

What can I do today to move my goals forward? List three things.

_____

_____

UPROOT
THE
UNNECESSARY

Uproot The Unnecessary

Imagine a beautiful flourishing rose garden. What place does trash, old bottles, or discarded cigarette butts have in this beautiful space? None. A wise gardener not only wants her space to display beauty but she ensures that nothing (internally) unnecessary is in the way of the growth inside of her prized space. A flourishing life rarely is filled with unnecessary things left to become distractions. Uprooting the unnecessary is to rid your life of things that detract from living life to the fullest. Unnecessary things can be grudge holding, limiting beliefs, poor habits, relationships that do not add value, or anything in the way of purposeful living. Remove the unnecessary blocking your optimal growth. Gardens and spaces where things grow usually need simple care. Life is much like a garden. It needs the right soil, time, patience, consistency, removal of unnecessary debris, and lots of love.

Uproot all the unnecessary things that have been in your life blocking you from abundance. You were designed to live an unlimited life.

Uproot the thoughts and practices in your life that are limiting you. Uproot anything between you and your new beginning.

When you are seeking change and undergoing spiritual and personal transformation there is uprooting that must take place in your heart, mind and soul to grow new things. Like a garden, our lives require pruning. Pruning removes overgrown roots or branches. Pruning increases growth and fruitfulness. Pruning allows us to grow something new for the new season we are entering.

What thoughts do you need to completely remove from your day-to-day thinking?

_____

_____

_____

What grudges do you need to let go of? Who do you need to forgive?

_____

_____

_____

What negative thoughts do you need to eradicate from your life?

_____

_____

_____

My prayer today:

_____

_____

_____

_____

Beautiful things grow in gardens because they are planted in the right soil and planted in the right season. Flourishing gardens receive the proper amount of sunlight, food, and are cared for consistently and properly maintained. With the same principle, we can flourish when we are rooted and planted properly.

What practices or tools do you need most right now to grow? (If you do not know, it is okay. Write "not sure" below. Your step is to then identify your challenge and then ask someone for support in that area.)

_____

_____

_____

My prayer today:

_____

_____

A pure and open heart makes way for unlimited blessings.

New beginnings are signaled by new mindsets. New mindsets grow from what is growing in your heart.

Old Mindsets I am uprooting from my life:

_____

_____

_____

My _New_ _Productive_ Mindsets that I am adopting:

_____

_____

_____

I will not allow distractions to block my blessings. I will not allow unforgiveness or bitterness to grow in the place where love was created to grow. I am forgiving:

_____   _____

_____   _____

Love and grace flows from my life.

"Transform your thoughts, transform your life."

Today, I set my mind and my heart to focus on:

_____

_____

_____

I am thankful for:

_____   _____

_____   _____

_____   _____

I am creating pleasant thoughts by focusing on:

_____

_____

My prayer today:

_____

_____

"New beginnings are often signaled by new mindsets."

My life is like a garden. I am abundant in good things. My life is filled with greatness and it multiplies over and over. I am <u>uprooting</u> these things that are in direct conflict with my growth and abundance:

_____

_____

_____

_____

I am creating a new routine in my life. As I cultivate the life I truly desire, I am making an intentional decision to reject anything in conflict with my growth, vision, authenticity, and my peace. I am welcoming these new experiences in my life:

_____

_____

_____

My actions are aligned with my vision for my life.

Healing is intentional.

I release every past disappointment. I am liberated. Today, I set my mind and my heart to focus on:

_____

_____

_____

_____

I am thankful for:

_____   _____

_____   _____

_____   _____

My prayer for today:

_____

_____

_____

My identity and life are not defined by my past disappointments and challenges.

I will no longer be weighed down by experiences in my life that were meant to distract me. Today, I declare that I am blessed, chosen, and moving forward.

I divorce myself from every false label, experience, and trauma from my past. I was created for a great purpose. I am fulfilling my purpose today.

Today, I set my mind and my heart to focus on:

_____

_____

I am thankful for:

_____   _____

_____   _____

_____   _____

My prayer for today:

_____

_____

Embrace your true identity, the one given to you by God.

Today I am praying for and extending grace to:

_____

_____

_____

My heart is open to receive:

_____

I am thankful for:

_____

_____

My prayer today is:

_____

_____

_____

What I focus on expands. I am expanding favor, grace, and love all around me.

Reflection

What am I feeling and thinking right now?

_____

_____

What lesson did I learn today?

_____

_____

How did I care for and/or invest in myself today?

_____

_____

What were my wins today?

_____

_____

What can I do today to move my goals forward? List three things.

_____

_____

MAKE
SPACE FOR
NEW THINGS

Make Space For New Things

Things, thoughts, old habits often fill our days and it eventually becomes our way of life. When we desire new things, new experiences, new levels, and a purposeful life there are changes that are required to meet those goals. In order to create new experiences in your life, you must make room for the desired experience and outcomes. Too often the desires we have for change get lost in translation because of our unwillingness to let go of old and unfruitful habits and mindsets. Our actions, words, and thoughts must align with the vision we have for the new stage we are entering.

In a garden, where good things grow in abundance, new things grow because there is pruning away of dead things that are in conflict with fruitfulness. Life is full when we make space for new things to grow.

Divorce yourself from past traumas and past disappointments. Do not allow past challenges to become your identity.

What is taking up space in your heart?

_____

_____

_____

What thoughts are leading your life? What words are creating your life?

_____

_____

_____

What thoughts do you need to completely remove from your day to day thinking?

_____

_____

_____

_____

Remember: Flourishing gardens require the right amount of sunlight.

How will you invest in yourself today?

_____

_____

_____

What old patterns are you breaking today?

_____

_____

_____

What dead issues, mindsets, behaviors need to be pruned from your life? What is in direct conflict with your growth?

_____

_____

_____

What steps do you need to take to move closer to your dreams? (If you are unsure, note that below and identify someone trusted that can help you determine some steps to support your goals.)

_____

_____

_____

My heart is open to receive:

_____

I am thankful for:

_____   _____

_____   _____

My prayer today is:

_____

_____

_____

Prepare for a new season, for new experience, release anything taking up space in your heart and mind.

Open your heart to new possibilities and opportunities.

Today, I set my mind and my heart to focus on:

_____

_____

Be open to something new, something different, a new season.

My heart is open to receive:

_____

I am thankful for:

_____   _____

_____   _____

_____   _____

My prayer for today:

_____

_____

Don't shrink back, evolve.

Today, I set my mind and my heart to focus on:

_____

_____

_____

I am thankful for:

_____   _____

_____   _____

_____   _____

I am growing and flourishing. I celebrate my growth in:

_____

My prayer for today:

_____

_____

_____

I deserve an unlimited life.

Today, I am thankful for:

_____

_____

I am not limited by rejection.
I am not limited by what I do not have.
I am not limited by anything.
I live an unlimited life.

In the past, what have you desired but believed you did not deserve?

_____

_____

I no longer limit myself. I was created to live an unlimited life. I am open and ready to receive:

_____

_____

_____

May he give you the desire of your heart and make all your plans succeed.
Psalm 20:4 NIV

Reflection

What am I feeling and thinking right now?

_____

_____

What lesson did I learn today?

_____

_____

How did I care for and/or invest in myself today?

_____

_____

What were my wins today?

_____

_____

What can I do today to move my goals forward? List three things.

_____

_____

CULTIVATE
A BEAUTIFUL
LIFE

Cultivate A Beautiful Life

Your focus and care will be required for whatever you are working towards. Whether it is changing an area of your life, creating new thought patterns, or reaching a goal cultivation is key. Whatever you desire will require as a space that has been cleared and made ready for the new things you are pursuing. Preparation may look like eliminating old limiting thoughts, identifying patterns in your life that you previously adopted, and being intentional about adopting new thoughts and actions. Whatever you pursue will require that you cultivate that area of your life so that whatever is growing can be maintained. Life is like a garden. What you focus on and prepare for matters.

It is also important to note that before you can cultivate a space you must survey it. Sometimes upon surveying the space we discover that major overhauling or excavation of the space is required before it is ready for a particular use. Excavating an area involves digging up things in order to learn what is happening under the surface. In life we can do the same. The blessing in surveying is discovering the challenges as well as the opportunities. If you believe you are starting over or starting from ground zero do not discount this. Far too often, people build upon spaces that have major issues underneath the surface. Check your perspective and continue on cultivating a great life and legacy. Starting over can be a blessing to do it better than the last time. This time start and stick to the work once you have surveyed the space and previous seasons (decisions, experiences, etc.) of your life.

Cultivate a beautiful life, grow good things, and allow those good things to grow in abundance. What are you cultivating? What is being developed in your life? Take time and really think about what you are growing in and with your life.

"He who cultivates his land
will have plenty of bread,
But he who follows worthless
people and frivolous pursuits
will have plenty of poverty."

Proverbs 28:19 AMP

What are you growing in your garden (in your heart, in your life)? What are you producing that will grow in abundance and positively impact your world but also the world around you? Take a moment to write your thoughts below.

_____

_____

_____

_____

What is your vision for your life? What do you desire your life and days to be filled with? Write it below.

_____

_____

_____

_____

Have you checked in lately on the progress of your vision? What do you need to move your goals forward?

_____

_____

_____

Are you struggling to make progress with your vision? Is this a God-sized vision?

_____

_____

_____

_____

In this chapter of your life, what are you cultivating? Is excavation required?

_____

_____

_____

_____

Cultivate New Mindsets

My intention for today is:

_____

As I cultivate a beautiful life, I am adopting a new mindset and vision for:

- _____

- _____

- _____

I am growing and flourishing. I celebrate my growth in:

_____

I am grateful for:

_____

My prayer for today:

_____

_____

New mindsets proceed new seasons.

Cultivate Your Vision

My intention for today:

_____

My top three goals for the next 21 days include:

1._____

2._____

3._____

To achieve these goals, I need to complete the following *steps*:

Goal 1_____

Goal 2_____

Goal 3_____

I am growing and cultivating:

_____

I am grateful for:

_____

The wise woman builds her house, but with her own hands the foolish one tears hers down. Proverbs 14:1 NIV

Cultivate Joy & Inner Beauty

My intention for today:

_____

I will discover joy in my life. My top three "joy-finding" goals for the next 21 days include:

- _____

- _____

- _____

I am discovering joy in:

_____

I choose to live a joy-filled life. I endeavor to **shift** my attitude and perspective about the following:

- _____

- _____

What matters is not your outer appearance—the styling of your hair, the jewelry you wear, the cut of your clothes—but your inner disposition. 1 Peter 3:4MSG

Cultivate: To improve, grow, or develop.

My intention for today:

_____

*I am thankful for every lesson and every win in my life, great and small.
Today, I celebrate:*

_____

_____

I am cultivating my life by improving:

- _____

- _____

- _____

My prayer for today:

_____

_____

*I am thankful for the distance I have come. I am thankful for the distance
I have yet to travel. I am thankful.*

Reflection

What am I feeling and thinking right now?

_____

_____

What lesson did I learn today?

_____

_____

How did I care for and/or invest in myself today?

_____

_____

What were my wins today?

_____

_____

What can I do today to move my goals forward? List three things.

_____

_____

INSERT
GRATITUDE

Insert Gratitude

Have you ever considered what resides in your heart and mind? What are the thoughts and words you use most?

Practicing honest introspection and evaluation of what we think, say, and do helps us determine what we really believe. Inserting gratitude into our daily lives helps us to increase and direct our attention on what is good and what is working for us. Increasing gratitude in our hearts produces greater vision for what is possible, solutions to challenges, and leads to abundance. Insert gratitude into the moments of your day and into the days of your life and watch how what is good grows. Allow gratitude to fill the spaces in your heart where there are voids and discontentment. Gratitude always leads us to abundance where we recognize we have more than enough.

How do you fill your days with gratitude?

The more you practice gratitude, the more you discover how much is working in your favor.

Joy is a choice.

Today, I will find joy in:

_____

My focus for today is:

_____

I am thankful for:

_____   _____

_____   _____

_____   _____

My heart is open to receive:

_____

I celebrate my growth in:

_____

My prayer for today:

_____

_____

"Gratitude is a powerful catalyst for happiness." -Amy Collette

Pause and prioritize gratitude.

I am grateful for:

_____   _____

_____   _____

_____   _____

_____   _____

_____   _____

*I prioritize love, peace, and joy in my life. I prioritize these **positive** thoughts over any negative ones:*

_____

_____

In cultivating a joyful life, I will incorporate these two practices and/or thoughts in my daily/morning routine:

- _____

- _____

Many things may compete for my attention, but peace, joy, love, and gratitude is my priority.

"*Whatever you focus on will expand.*"

*Allow yourself 2-5 minutes of **uninterrupted time** for this activity. List as many things as you can.*

I am expanding my focus and gratitude for:

_____

_____

_____

_____

_____

_____

_____

_____

_____

"Gratitude turns what we have into enough." – Anonymous.

When gratitude preoccupies the heart not much else can.

My intention for today:

_____

What are some things that concern you and are not desirable currently in your life?

_____

_____

Now, create positive declarations and gratitude-based statements for what you <u>do</u> desire?

_____

_____

_____

Gratitude and thanksgiving have the power to change the perspective we have of our current situations.

Reflection

What am I feeling and thinking right now?

_____

_____

What lesson did I learn today?

_____

_____

How did I care for and/or invest in myself today?

_____

_____

What were my wins today?

_____

_____

What can I do today to move my goals forward? List three things.

_____

_____

LIVE BIG

Live Big

Life is a gift. With the time we have been given, we should seek to live to our fullest potential. Why not live big? Live big and experience all that you were created for.

Live big.

Do not settle.

Do not shrink.

"You must decide if you are going to rob the world or bless it with the rich, valuable, potent, untapped resources locked away within you."

– **Myles Munroe**

There are <u>no</u> limits.

Today, I set my mind and my heart to focus on:

_____

_____

Three limitations that I am removing from my thinking:

1. _____

2. _____

3. _____

I am thankful for:

_____

My prayer today:

_____

_____

_____

I am unstoppable.

Live your vision.

My Vision (Write your vision).

_____

_____

_____

_____

_____

_____

_____

My prayer over my vision:

_____

_____

_____

_____

I am capable. I am able. I will reach my goals.

To live my vision, I am planting and growing these things in my garden:

_____

_____

_____

Today, I will grow in these areas of my life:

_____

_____

_____

My prayer today over my goals is:

_____

_____

_____

I am a success.

I live an unlimited life.

My intention for today:

_____

I live purposefully.
My vision is clear.
I value time and make great use of it.
I serve my gifts as God directs me to.
God leads me down a flourishing path.

I am fully convinced that I will _____.

I confident that I will _____.

I am committed to my success, I will _____.

God is committed to my success, I can _____.

I can. I will. I must _____.

Today's Prayer

God created me to succeed. I choose to live in the image of God. I am not limited by any circumstance. I was born to do great things and to make a great impact. I live an abundant, unlimited life. Amen.

Live big.

I will live boldly. I will boldly live my dreams by:

_____

_____

_____

_____

My dreams and desires are to:

_____

_____

_____

Today, I am thankful to God for:

_____

_____

My prayer today:

_____

_____

I live in the vision God has planted in my heart.

Dreams are to be lived.

Today, I will invest in my dreams by:

_____

_____

_____

I will continue to pursue the big dreams God has planted in my heart. My big dreams are to:

_____

_____

_____

_____

I am <u>no</u> longer fearful of:

_____

My prayer today:

_____

_____

I trust God. My full confidence is in God's promises.

Reflection

What am I feeling and thinking right now?

_____

_____

What lesson did I learn today?

_____

_____

How did I care for and/or invest in myself today?

_____

_____

What were my wins today?

_____

_____

What can I do today to move my goals forward? List three things.

_____

_____

EMBRACE GOD'S DESIGN

Embrace God's Design

Too often our lives become so permeated by external influences that we assume identities that God **never** intended for us. Past hurts, challenges, environments do not dictate who we are. These things certainly do not dictate our God-design. However, far too often many external things distort our vision of how God sees us and the purpose for which He has created us. When we embrace our God-design we find clarity, embrace purpose, and pursue the paths that align with who God has predestined us to be.

To embrace your God-design you must become acquainted with God. God is the ultimate Creator. Everything and every person He designed He did so with an excellent purpose in mind. He only creates greatness. To embrace your God-design you have to zero in on The Creator who formed you.

For you created my inmost being;
*   you knit me together in my mother's womb.*

I praise you because I am fearfully and wonderfully made;
*   your works are wonderful,*
*   I know that full well.*

My frame was not hidden from you when I was made in the secret place,
*   when I was woven together in the depths of the earth.*

Your eyes saw my unformed body;
*   all the days ordained for me were written in your book*
*   before one of them came to be.   Psalm 139:13-16*

"You were designed to win."

I am validated by God.

God saw everything that He had made, and behold, it was very good and He validated it completely. –Genesis 1:31a AMP

Pause. Take time here to bask in the beauty of God's presence. Turn your thoughts off and make your heart available to God your Creator. Be open. Be attentive. Be meditative of goodness. Rest in the beauty of God.

Use the space below to ask God questions at the beginning of your listening session. Take notes of what God is saying to you.

_____

_____

_____

_____

_____

_____

God desires that you know His heart and thoughts toward you. His thoughts are very good toward you.

I agree with God.

My intention for today:

_____

Below write powerful thoughts and attributes about yourself. What are your strengths? What are you becoming better in? This activity may take some time to complete. A good place to discover who God says you are can be found in scriptures in the Bible. Also, consider your attributes that sometimes feel challenging (ie. being vocal, sometimes this and other attributes are indicators of a greater purpose in your life. Perhaps you are an advocate for others.) Use this activity to identify your unique design.

I am _____.   I am _____.

I am _____.   I am _____.

I am _____.   I am _____.

I am _____.   I am _____.

I am _____.   I am _____.

I am _____.   I am _____.

I am _____.   I am _____.

I agree with who God says I am and who He has designed and purposed me to be.

You were designed for accomplishment, engineered for success, and endowed with the seeds of greatness. -Zig Ziglar

My intention for today:

_____

What have you been called to do with your life? What is your declaration?

_____

_____

_____

I thank God for:

_____

_____

My prayer today is:

_____

_____

_____

You are purpose in living form.

I belong to God.

It does not matter who does not accept or embrace you. You belong to God. You matter to God.

Take a moment here and in the space below list all of the reasons why you matter to God. Really connect to God's love for you.

_____

_____

_____

_____

Today, I open my heart to God, who accepts and blesses me. I let go of every experience where I experienced rejection.

I let go of:

_____

_____

My prayer today:

_____

_____

The Lord is my shepherd, I lack nothing. Psalm 23:1 NIV

Life Is Full

My life is full of blessings. My life is full because God's thoughts towards me are beautiful. God sees me as:

_____

_____

_____

_____

I am grateful for:

_____

_____

My prayer today:

_____

_____

_____

God is my source. Nothing can stop the fullness of my life. My future is secured in the hands of God.

I embrace my God-design.

My intention for today:

_____

I am grateful for:

_____

What unique gifts has God given you? (Think about the things you do naturally over and over. Think about what you are passionate about and what brings you joy, and consider what your friends say you do really well.)

_____

_____

What do you love about who God has made you to be?

_____

_____

Today's Prayer

I embrace my unique God-design. I know that I was created to make the world better. I am created to conquer every challenge and to break barriers. I am liberated from every false identity outside of who God says I am. I embrace God's goodness and all of who He has created me to be.

Reflection

What am I feeling and thinking right now?

_____

_____

What lesson did I learn today?

_____

_____

How did I care for and/or invest in myself today?

_____

_____

What were my wins today?

_____

_____

What can I do today to move my goals forward? List three things.

_____

_____

Dear Self....

Write a letter to your younger self or your future self. What do you want to say? What do you need to say to yourself?

_____

_____

_____

_____

_____

_____

_____

_____

_____

_____

_____

Dear God....

Write a letter or a prayer to God. What questions do you have of God? Ask them. What thanksgiving do you want to give to God? Write it.

_____

_____

_____

_____

_____

_____

_____

_____

_____

_____

_____

_____

Closing

Life is full of whatever we decide to fill it with. The God who created you only has good things in mind for you. Wherever you are in your life journey my prayer is that you will recognize that you were designed to live an unlimited life, designed for a beautiful purpose, and that you never settle for an unfulfilled life.

Everyday that God has granted comes with an opportunity to discover the purpose assigned to that day and to our lives. Life is full of some experiences that are exceptionally hard to understand, never allow those experiences to deter you from the greatness you were created to experience and live in. Fill your days with love and gratitude as you embrace God's purpose for your life.

Like a garden, take great care of the life God has given you and serve the abundance of what you grow from it with the world around you.

Let's grow,
Cassandra

Notes

Notes

_____

_____

_____

_____

_____

_____

_____

_____

_____

_____

_____

_____

Reflection

What am I feeling and thinking right now?

_____

_____

What lesson did I learn today?

_____

_____

How did I care for and/or invest in myself today?

_____

_____

What were my wins today?

_____

_____

What can I do today to move my goals forward? List three things.

_____

_____

Reflection

What am I feeling and thinking right now?

_____

_____

What lesson did I learn today?

_____

_____

How did I care for and/or invest in myself today?

_____

_____

What were my wins today?

_____

_____

What can I do today to move my goals forward? List three things.

_____

_____

Reflection

What am I feeling and thinking right now?

_____

_____

What lesson did I learn today?

_____

_____

How did I care for and/or invest in myself today?

_____

_____

What were my wins today?

_____

_____

What can I do today to move my goals forward? List three things.

_____

_____

About The Book

When you are experiencing growth and transition in your life one excellent tool to make use of is journaling. Journaling with intention can be transformative. What happens when you need to gain a fresh perspective on life? When you need to refresh your thinking and replace unproductive thoughts with new life-giving thoughts? The *Life Is Full Journal* helps users to put a pause to the overwhelm and engage their deepest desires for a fulfilled life. Engaging your truest thoughts and desires often leads to greater clarity. *Life Is Full Journal* creates a space where users can clarify their thoughts and move toward their vision. First readers are encouraged to strip away the noise by answering reflective questions, adopting gratitude as a daily tool, and getting to the heart of what is good and true about their lives.

The *Life Is Full Journal* is a resource for anyone seeking purposeful daily reflection. This journal can be used as a compliment to the book, *Life Is Full: Musings on The Beauty of Life, Growth, and Love* or used as a stand alone resource. Life Is Full Journal users will enjoy writing prompts designed to cultivate gratitude.

About The Author

Cassandra is an emerging thought leader poised to reach millions of readers experiencing life transitions with a message of hope. Cassandra desires to support others as they embrace their God-design and live a fulfilled life.

Cassandra N. Vincent is a certified personal and executive coach and transformational speaker on a mission to lead a movement of happy and whole women who are committed to leading with purpose. Driven by her personal story of challenge and triumph, her messages are soaked in themes of empowerment, personal development and growth.

Cassandra is a dynamic communicator who speaks from a place of compassion, transparency, and authenticity, making her an in-demand speaker and facilitator.

Thanks to her unique ability to help audiences change the way they see themselves and their lives, Cassandra's talks and signature event, "The Vision + Strategy Brunch" are truly transformational. Her gift lies in helping women create a vision for their lives.

Cassandra is the author of *Life Is Full: Musings on The Beauty of Life, Growth, and Love* and *The Smart Woman's Bounce Back Guide After a Bad Breakup.*

For more information visit www.cassandranvincent.com

or email info@cassandranvincent.com

www.ingramcontent.com/pod-product-compliance
Lightning Source LLC
LaVergne TN
LVHW061330060426
835513LV00015B/1343